First
Teeline
Workbook

First Teeline Workbook

REVISED EDITION

I.C. Hill and Meriel Bowers

Heinemann Educational Books

London

Heinemann Educational Books Ltd
22 Bedford Square, London WC1B 3HH

LONDON   EDINBURGH   MELBOURNE   AUCKLAND
HONG KONG   SINGAPORE   KUALA LUMPUR   NEW DELHI
IBADAN   NAIROBI   JOHANNESBURG
EXETER (NH)   KINGSTON   PORT OF SPAIN

British Library Cataloguing in Publication Data
Hill, I. C.
  First Teeline workbook.—2nd rev. ed.
  1. Shorthand—Teeline—Problems, exercises, etc
  I. Title   II. Bowers, Meriel
  653'.428   Z56.2.T4

ISBN 0-435-45345-9

Filmset in 'Monophoto' Ehrhardt
by Eta Services (Typesetters) Ltd., Beccles, Suffolk
Printed in Great Britain by Biddles Ltd, Guildford

Contents

Preface

This book has been planned as a follow-up book for Teeline writers who have completed the theory or as a supplementary book for those using *Teeline Revised Edition*.

It should be particularly useful for those attending a second-year evening class or who, for various reasons, wish to review the system while trying to increase speed.

Teeline outlines have been kept to a minimum because it is expected that by the time this book is used, individual writing styles will have been developed. Checking should be done by reading, writing or typing back from Teeline notes. Timed reading and timed transcription are useful exercises.

In Chapters 3 to 21 outlines for difficult words have been provided on dotted lines in the left-hand margin. Dotted lines have also been provided elsewhere in case students wish to write in outlines for other words. If teachers do not wish their students to write in the book instructions should be given to this effect.

For ease of dictating the passages have been divided into 10-word lines, thus facilitating reading at any speed. The numbers in brackets at the end of each exercise refer to the total number of words.

Teeline Word List can be used for reference in any cases where the writer needs outline guidance.

I. C. Hill and M. Bowers
February 1983

Notes to Students

The purpose of learning Teeline is to use it. Teeline learning should, therefore, be looked upon mainly as training for whatever objective you hope your study will eventually help you to achieve.

When reading Teeline, always trace over the outlines with a pen or pencil, not making any mark, but getting the feel of the outlines. This helps to develop fluency in writing.

Never copy an outline without thinking or saying it. If you can work in a room on your own, say the words quietly to yourself. The more writing, copying and drilling you can do, the more automatic will be your response in producing a readable outline when you try writing from dictation. Plenty of practice makes perfect!

Longhand exercises provide valuable preparation for dictation. After you have put them into Teeline, make sure you check them carefully. For guidance, *Teeline Word List* or the relevant theory unit in *Teeline Revised Edition* can be consulted, but a few outlines likely to cause writing difficulty are included and these can be used for preliminary practice or recognition drill.

Remember that the outlines given in this book, and in other Teeline books, are recommended outlines, but they are not necessarily the only acceptable outlines. You may wish to add vowels to make reading back easier, or to shorten outlines when you become familiar with words, or when they are in sentences that make their meanings absolutely clear; but it is better to write a longer outline and to read it back correctly than to contract it and misread it when transcribing.

New or unfamiliar words should be written in full by building them up as you hear them spoken. When reading back, you can then decide what is a good way of shortening the outline if this is desirable. If you cannot manage to put down a full outline, get something down, even if it is only the initial letter, rather than leave a gap in your notes.

Never rub out mistakes. You will not have time to do this when taking dictation. Instead, quickly and neatly cross out, or ring the error and write the correct outline next to it.

It is useful to have a margin in your notebook so that, when checking, correct outlines can be written in the margin on the same line as the ringed error.

It is also a useful exercise from time to time to see if you can read Teeline notes that were taken several days previously. We call these 'cold notes' and if you can read them back easily, then there is nothing wrong with your Teeline.

Finally, keep a vocabulary notebook in which you can list all new words, or those you spell wrongly, with their meanings and the Teeline outlines. You can buy or make a notebook with an alphabetical index, so that it is easy to look up any particular word you require. Now and then, pick out one page and practise the words on it. This will help you to build up the wide knowledge of words which it is necessary for a successful shorthand writer to have.

I Sentences Involving the Teeline Alphabet and Joinings

Put the following sentences into Teeline and then try reading or transcribing them from your notes:

1

.... Will you be able to go to their show this (*10*)

.... year? It is very good. (*15*)

2

.... We shall go to see the accident damage to the (*10*)

.... car and hear how it happened. (*16*)

3

.... If it is a fine day, I shall go to (*10*)

.... meet them as the walk will do me good. (*19*)

4

.... The teacher told us that in her view they are (*10*)

.... quite able to climb to the top of the hill. (*20*)

5

.... It must have been very annoying when you missed the (*10*)

.... bus and had to wait thirty minutes in the cold. (*20*)

6

.... Kindliness and good manners cost nothing, but they help to (*10*)

.... add happiness to life and make it easier to bear. (*20*)

7

.... The college opened today. The teacher showed us how to (*10*)

.... do Teeline. We like it and will use it to (20)

.... make notes. (22)

8

.... I like the view from the top of the hill, (10)

.... but it is chilly up there, so we shall not (20)

.... go up today. (23)

9

.... Gossip is generally accepted to be a bad thing but (10)

.... we all indulge in it at times, and most of (20)

.... us enjoy it! (23)

10

.... This is where the road narrows, so it will be (10)

.... necessary to get into a (single) line until we have (20)

.... passed the church. (23)

11

.... I hear you had an accident in the car. Is (10)

.... it damaged? If it is, you will have to take (20)

.... it into the garage. (24)

12

.... How soon will you be able to make me a (10)

.... (cup of tea) I am very cold and I should (20)

.... also like something to eat. (25)

13

.... I hope you will visit us when you are in (10)

.... the city. We are within walking distance of the square (20)

.... and quite near the railway museum. (26)

14

.... The woman wished to buy two pieces of (yellow) velvet, (10)

.... but the manageress was in no hurry to serve her (20)

.... so she left the shop in disgust. (27)

15

.... I shall have to wait and see if we go (10)

.... to the shop that day. If so, we shall not (20)

.... be able to manage to meet him. (27)

16

.... It may not be the biggest, but (in my opinion) (10)

.... it is the best magazine of its kind and I (20)

.... should be very sorry to see the end of it. (30)

17

.... We had your message and note that the office meeting (10)

.... is not being held at one o'clock, but at a (20)

.... time to be decided by the head of the department. (30)

18

.... Sally is making dolls in her spare time. If you (10)

.... go to the sale in the church hall on Tuesday, (20)

.... you will be able to see some of them there. (30)

19

.... According to the Chairman, sales are well behind what we (10)

.... had estimated. We do not know why this should be (20)

.... so, but we must find out what has caused it. (30)

20

.... The watchers on the jetty had a good view of (10)

.... the vessel as it sailed out of the harbour, and (20)

.... waved to those on board until they lost sight of (30)

.... it. (31)

21

.... Sue is going to buy a small car to help (10)

.... her get about easily. She is a good way from (20)

.... the office and the shops and there is a very (30)

.... poor bus service. (33)

22

.... The car I hope to get will be kept in (10)

.... the garage. I have electric light in there, so I (20)

.... will be able to check the engine while the car (30)

.... is in the garage. (34)

23

.... The boy kept some pet rabbits in hutches in a (10)

c......... shed (Each day,) when he had finished school, he used (20)

.... to go to feed them. Once a week, he cleaned (30)

.... out their hutches and sometimes he let them out in (40)

.... the yard where they seemed quite happy. (47)

24

.... Last year we had a lovely holiday. It was very (10)

.... hot and we spent a lot of time in the (20)

.... swimming pool. We are not yet able to dive in (30)

.... at the deep end, but we had fun at the (40)

.... shallow end and managed to swim across the pool by (50)

.... the end of the week. (55)

2   Alphabetical Sentences for Repetition Drill

Put into Teeline and type or read back:

1

.... Alan and I may be going away again in August.   (*10*)

2

.... He always answers the letters as soon as he is   (*10*)

.... able.   (*11*)

3

.... Your beach ball is bigger than mine, so it will   (*10*)

.... be the best one to take with us.   (*18*)

4

.... I am going to buy a bottle of this beauty   (*10*)

.... lotion at the shop.   (*14*)

5

.... The cost of coffee rises if there is a bad   (*10*)

.... harvest in any year.   (*14*)

6

.... The police closed a section of the road where the   (*10*)

.... cycle race was being held.   (*15*)

7

.... As the boys dipped their hands in the pond, the   (*10*)

.... tadpoles darted about, making it difficult to catch them.   (*19*)

8

.... I saw him digging a deep hole where he buried (*10*)

.... a bundle and deduced it must be the missing cash. (*20*)

9

.... It is difficult to estimate the effects of the department's (*10*)

.... latest education bill. (*13*)

10

.... In this edition of the science book, there is a (*10*)

.... different equation at the bottom of page two. (*18*)

11

.... The reason Emily has so little energy is that she (*10*)

.... does not eat enough, especially of the energy-giving foods. (*20*)

12

.... The fisherman decided to build a fire and cook the (*10*)

.... biggest fish. It was getting late and he was ready (*20*)

.... to eat something. (*23*)

13

.... The electric fans must be finished to fit in with (*10*)

.... the date of the festival. (*15*)

14

.... If you wish to show your goodwill, I suggest you (*10*)

.... give a generous gift to the general hospital. (*18*)

15

.... The garage made a good job of my car, although   (10)

.... it was badly damaged when I took it to them.   (20)

16

.... We may be able to send you a home help   (10)

.... when you are well enough to leave hospital.   (18)

17

.... As was their habit, when they reached the heath, they   (10)

.... opened their hamper and ate the food heartily.   (18)

18

.... Harry was always in a hurry to get away from   (10)

.... the office to see how well he could handle the   (20)

.... horse he had been lent.   (25)

19

.... Some illnesses are caused by ignorance and some are

                    [imaginary,   (10)

.... but if individuals are immunized, they are less likely to   (20)

.... catch some diseases.   (23)

20

.... The inquest showed that the Italian had died from a   (10)

.... heart attack which happened when he had been in a   (20)

.... fight with an Irishman.   (24)

21

.... Jamaica is the name of an island in the West   (*10*)

.... Indies where rum is made and enjoyed.   (*17*)

22

.... The Japanese use chopsticks to eat some of their food.   (*10*)

.... Not many who live in the West are good at   (*20*)

.... using chopsticks.   (*22*)

23

.... Finding an old kettle in the kitchen of the deserted   (*10*)

.... house near the lake, they managed to light a fire   (*20*)

.... and then made some tea.   (*25*)

24

.... In the past, kings had to keep their kingdoms by   (*10*)

.... killing their enemies. In those days, no attempt was made   (*20*)

.... ' to be kind to them.   (*25*)

25

.... The lady climbed the hill and saw the little lambs   (*10*)

.... dotted about on the landscape below, and thought how lovely   (*20*)

.... they looked.   (*22*)

26

.... It is the job of a Justice of the Peace   (*10*)

.... to sentence those who do not keep the law of   (*20*)

.... the land.   (*22*)

27

.... It was a mistake to let the mastiff eat all (*10*)

.... the liver. It is a massive dog and it will (*20*)

.... soon be barking again, but there is nothing left to (*30*)

.... give it. (*32*)

28

.... In a minute the meal will be ready, so will (*10*)

.... you add a little milk to the mushroom sauce? (*19*)

29

.... My niece is packing her knapsack. She is taking a (*10*)

.... boat to Norway where she hopes to find a nursing (*20*)

.... job. (*21*)

30

.... I could not help noticing how thin and badly nourished (*10*)

.... he looked, but not knowing him very well, I was (*20*)

.... nervous of mentioning it. (*24*)

31

.... In my opinion, they should observe the official rules and (*10*)

.... obey the officers. (*13*)

32

.... The needles should go into the oblong box and the (*10*)

.... odd pins in the oval one. (*16*)

33

.... The puppy pushed its nose into my palm and held (*10*)

.... up its paw in an attempt to make me notice (*20*)

.... it was carrying the paper. (*25*)

34

.... At the inn we ate a meal of pigeon and (*10*)

.... potato pie with pickles and a steamed pudding. This was (*20*)

.... designed to keep out the cold, but not to reduce (*30*)

.... weight. (*31*)

35

.... One rarely hears these days of quince jam, but years (*10*)

.... ago, it used to be quite a delicacy. (*18*)

36

.... The men queued up at the bar ready to quaff (*10*)

.... their beer, but the barmaid was equipped with a quick (*20*)

.... wit which could deal with their quips. (*27*)

37

.... Much of the railway's rolling stock is reported to be (*10*)

.... in need of repair, but the money required to put (*20*)

.... things right is not there. (*25*)

38

.... The girls raved about the record made by their favourite (*10*)

.... pop singer, but to Rachael it seemed only a raucous (*20*)

.... row. (*21*)

39

.... They sat in silence on the soft sands in the (*10*)

.... sunshine. The sea was smooth and it was safe to (*20*)

.... swim in the bay on such a day. (*28*)

40

.... Despite medical advice it is still surprising how stupid we (*10*)

.... are. We smoke and eat too many sweets and take (*20*)

.... too much sugar and then we are surprised when we (*30*)

.... are sick. (*32*)

41

.... The teacher told the class to sketch the tulips but (*10*)

.... not to touch them. (*14*)

42

.... If you take a telescope and twist the top, you (*10*)

.... will be able to see many things in space. (*19*)

43

.... There was uproar at the umpire's decision, and it took (*10*)

.... some time to silence the onlookers. (*16*)

44

.... The issue being discussed by the unions was settled by (*10*)

.... an unanimous vote and an ugly situation was thereby avoided. (*20*)

45

.... As the vicar and the curate put on their vestments, (*10*)

.... they heard an odd noise issuing from the vault of (20)

.... the church. (22)

46

.... This velvet is very good value, and it is very (10)

.... high fashion at the moment. I like the vivid shades (20)

.... best. (21)

47

.... Equal pay is supposed to be the law, but women (10)

.... do not always get the same wages as men although (20)

.... they may be doing the same jobs. (27)

48

.... The wasp was caught in the web and weakly waved (10)

.... its wings, but it was a wasted effort as it (20)

.... was not able to escape. (25)

49

.... The yacht is a light sailing vessel used in races. (10)

.... There are many yachting clubs and it is lovely to (20)

.... see the boats, with their red, yellow and blue sails (30)

.... blowing as they glide by. (35)

50

.... The eldest of the three youths lives in Yorkshire. He (10)

.... is hoping to go to Yugoslavia this year, but he (20)

.... has to have a visa from the Passport Office. (29)

51

.... Additional classes in yoga, yodelling and making yoghurt are [being (10)

.... put on this year at the local night school. (19)

52

.... In England, zebras are seen only in the zoo, but (10)

.... they are not as savage as lions and tigers. (19)

53

.... Zoe got lost in the maze, but yelled until she (10)

.... was discovered. (12)

54

.... A bottle of champagne was opened and all joined in (10)

.... toasting the champion and wishing him well. (17)

55

.... The choral society gave a cheque to the hospital. They (10)

.... had collected the money by singing at local chapels and (20)

.... churches. (21)

56

.... The shark shot from the shadow of the boat to (10)

.... attack the swimming boy, but the men managed to scare (20)

.... it away by shouting at it. (26)

57

.... The *Taming of the Shrew* by Shakespeare was made into (10)

.... a musical show called *Kiss me Kate*. (17)

58

.... The thief was thirsty so he took three bottles of   (*10*)

.... sherry from the thatched cottage when he raided ɩ.   (*19*)

59

.... In theory it is a good thing to be thrifty,   (*10*)

.... but today it seems to pay to throw your money   (*20*)

.... away instead of saving it.   (*25*)

60

.... Who gave the bottle of whisky, which was the main   (*10*)

.... prize, to raise funds at the Wheatsheaf Hotel dance?   (*19*)

61

.... While the game of whist was going on, Beryl whispered   (*10*)

.... that this gave us a chance to make the phone   (*20*)

.... call, whereupon we slipped out of the hall.   (*28*)

3 The F Blends

I

...🖊.... The man wished to buy his wife a fur coat, (10)

..🖊...... but could not afford it. (15)

2

🖊...🖊. Half the road had been flooded and the night frost (10)

🖊...🖊. had caused icy patches to form on its surface. (19)

3

🖊...🖊 We had a useful and peaceful meeting and I am (10)

...🖊.... hopeful that this will be the first of many such (20)

.....🖊. occasions. (21)

4

..🖊.... I had a small bottle of French perfume bought for (10)

🖊.🖊 my birthday, which I shall use carefully to make it (20)

.... last. (21)

5

...🖊.... My friend had the good luck to make a flight (10)

🖊...... to the States and while there she acquired a taste (20)

.🖊.... for waffles. (22)

6

.🖊... Upon reflection, I realized that in my haste, I forgot (10)

.... to tell my friend where I should meet her for (20)

.... lunch on Friday. (23)

7

A burst of clapping followed the famous singer's recital. It (*10*)

was difficult to believe he was almost forty, as he (*20*)

still looked very youthful. (*24*)

8

Freepost is a Post Office service whereby firms may pay (*10*)

in advance to receive an answer from clients in response (*20*)

to a newspaper advertisement. (*24*)

9

His wife does not usually buy raffle tickets, but today (*10*)

she was lucky and the prize was a box of (*20*)

frozen foods, which has filled the freezer for them. (*29*)

10

From the first, it had been fairly obvious that the (*10*)

statement made against the firm was false and that it (*20*)

would be a farce to go on with the court (*30*)

action. (*31*)

4   The T and D Blends

1

.... The boys trespassed in the cornfield as they searched for   (*10*)

.... their fox terrier, which had disappeared while chasing a rabbit.   (*20*)

2

.... It is really appalling that the modernization of the drainage   (*10*)

.... system has had to be abandoned because the official monetary   (*10*)

.... backing has not materialized.   (*24*)

3

.... The torrential storms of the past few days caused damage   (*10*)

.... in many streets, and the fire service had to pump   (*20*)

.... much flood water away.   (*24*)

4

.... There is always a good deal of hard effort needed   (*10*)

.... on the part of a gardener to keep hedges neatly   (*20*)

.... cut and the beds free from weeds.   (*27*)

5

.... The trading estate is being built on the western side   (*10*)

.... of the city away from the shopping parades and almost   (*20*)

.... opposite two factories which are already in use.   (*28*)

6

.... The lecturer built up a true picture of the history   (*10*)

.... of the theatre in England from the days of gas (20)

.... lighting on the stage to today's modern electrical equipment. (29)

7

.... Dear Madam, In order to keep the correspondence records up (10)

.... to date, will you let me have your daughter's address (20)

.... as I believe she has gone to training college? Yours (30)

.... faithfully. (31)

8

.... The train was full and, at first, we stood in (10)

.... the corridor, but then we managed to find a seat (20)

.... in the dining section, where we obtained a refreshing cup (30)

.... of tea. (32)

9

.... The elm tree has been afflicted during the past few (10)

.... years by Dutch elm disease, which causes the wood to (20)

.... decay and go rotten, the tree later having to be (30)

.... destroyed by felling. (33)

10

.... In order to reach championship standard, sportsmen and

[sportswomen must (10)

.... go into serious training, which requires tremendous dedication

[on their (20)

.... part. They are often out on the track going through (30)

.... their routines early in the day, while most of us (40)

.... are still sleeping. (43)

5   The LR, MR and WR Blends

1

Firms specializing in remaking old-fashioned pine wardrobes
[have discovered   (*10*)

a ready market for them in America.   (*17*)

2

At one time, roller skating used to be a popular   (*10*)

sport, but today ice skating seems to attract more attention.   (*20*)

3

It is customary when learning Teeline to rule a margin   (*10*)

in the notebook so that alterations to the shorthand notes   (*20*)

may be written clearly.   (*24*)

4

or. The smaller of the two summer chalets has been much   (*10*)

admired by all the viewing clients, but no one has   (*20*)

yet offered the reserve selling price.   (*26*)

5

As the summer wore on, he suddenly realized he was   (*10*)

without a friend in the world, in a foreign land   (*20*)

and with rumours of a war in the neighbouring colony.   (*30*)

6

The colour film I started last summer still has not   (*10*)

been used. If it is fine tomorrow, I will take   (*20*)

...e.... some pictures of the flower beds in the park to (30)

....../.... use up the remaining shots. (35)

7

....⟋.... It is said that worry and not work causes weariness, (10)

.... but what is worse than waking each morning, knowing that (20)

.... one is going to spend the day doing work in (30)

....⟋.... which one has no real satisfaction. (36)

8

...⟋.... In years gone by, ladies used metal curlers to put (10)

...⟋.... a wave in their hair. Later on, coloured rollers were (20)

...⟋.... popular, but today both of these have largely gone out (30)

.... of use because more natural styles are the fashion. (39)

9

.⟋.... If we were to leave work early we could be (10)

..V.... at the hardware shop within half an hour. I am (20)

⟋.⟋.... particularly keen to buy a rotary mower, so that we (30)

.... shall be able to clear the land for cultivation at (40)

.ع.... the end of the allotment. (45)

10

...ς.... Mary liked to have a shower as soon as she (10)

...⟋.... woke in the morning. Mark had to rush off to (20)

...⟋.... work straight after a hasty slice of toast and marmalade, (30)

.... so he liked to take a warm bath when he (40)

...⟋.... returned home, to soothe his weariness before going to bed. (50)

6   Vowel Indicators as Word Endings

1

[shorthand] The shadows lengthened as we crossed the meadow, and the   (*10*)

[shorthand] sun sank slowly behind the hills.   (*16*)

2

[shorthand] I had no idea he was such a good singer.   (*10*)

[shorthand] He reaches the high notes seemingly without effort.   (*18*)

3

[shorthand] When the ship sank, nine men saved their lives by   (*10*)

[shorthand] clinging to bits of the wreckage until a small boat   (*20*)

[shorthand] rescued them.   (*22*)

4

[shorthand] The bank manager blinked in astonishment when the young

                                       [man   (*10*)

[shorthand] told him how much money he wished to borrow on   (*20*)

[shorthand] a long-term basis.   (*23*)

5

[shorthand] Are you sure that no one saw you give him   (*10*)

[shorthand] the letter? If anyone did, it would be difficult to   (*20*)

[shorthand] keep things quiet any longer.   (*25*)

6

[shorthand] As it was market day, the entire length of the   (*10*)

[shorthand] high street was thronged with shoppers, so it was easy   (*20*)

[shorthand] for the detective to mingle with them.   (*27*)

7

.... I think you should be quite frank when you answer (*10*)

[shorthand] their questions. They have a thankless task and need all (*20*)

.... the help you are able to give them. (*28*)

8

[shorthand] Will you help me to untangle these hanks of pink (*10*)

.... wool? I think there will be enough to make a (*20*)

[shorthand] jumper from them to fit the child's toy monkey. (*29*)

9

[shorthand] I worried for a long time in case my pink (*10*)

[shorthand] woollen sweater would shrink in the wash, so I am (*20*)

[shorthand] thankful I followed the directions enclosed in the package as (*30*)

[shorthand] *or* [shorthand] the sweater is still the right size. (*37*)

10

[shorthand] Have you seen the tanker which is said to be (*10*)

[shorthand] sinking at the end of the pier? What do you (*20*)

[shorthand] think was the cause of the accident? Some say it (*30*)

.... ran into the pier and that there will be an (*40*)

[shorthand] enquiry to find out why. This is the first time (*50*)

[shorthand] that I have heard of a ship being wrecked off (*60*)

.... this coast. (*62*)

7 General Review Exercises (1)

Put into Teeline and type or read back:

1

Does this information make any difference to them? *(8)*

2

Of course, it is my intention to go to the *(10)*

football match with you. *(14)*

3

We were each going to buy one of these books, *(10)*

but there was only one left. *(16)*

4

Last time I was in the department store, they had *(10)*

only a few of those cards on show. *(18)*

5

Why was no reference made to the letter that we *(10)*

sent to the Chairman of the Board last week? *(19)*

6

Almost half the Members of Parliament voted in favour of *(10)*

the Finance Bill, but the government was defeated by three *(20)*

votes. *(21)*

7

I am more or less satisfied that they are telling *(10)*

..*shorthand*.. the truth but I need more information in order to (20)

.... be sure. (22)

8

..*shorthand*.... We have had some difficulty in obtaining a reference for (10)

..*shorthand*.... Mr Fowler, as the director of his firm is on (20)

..*shorthand*..... a tour of the Far East. (26)

9

..*shorthand*.. Referring to the firm's financial statement, I am sure you (10)

.... will agree that while this has been a difficult year, (20)

.... they have, in fact, done fairly well. (27)

10

....*shorthand*.... My friends are hoping to modernize the cottage they have (10)

.... bought but they will not be able to attend to (20)

..*shorthand*..*shorthand* this straight away. Such things take time. (27)

11

..*shorthand*.... I am sorry to hear that the Chairman is not (10)

..*shorthand*.... as well as he might be, and I hope that (20)

...*shorthand*.... before long he will be feeling more lively. (28)

12

——*shorthand* May we draw your attention to the fact that you (10)

...*shorthand*.... have not yet settled your bill of 14 February? We (20)

..*shorthand*..... should be glad to have your cheque for this at (30)

...*shorthand*... once. (31)

Prepare the following for dictation:

13

It is difficult to imagine what life was like before (*10*)

there were any telephones. Today they are so much a (*20*)

part of our lives that most of us would feel (*30*)

quite lost without them. (*34*)

14

The social club has had some difficulty in getting a (*10*)

party together to visit the Houses of Parliament, so it (*20*)

has been decided to do something quite different, but we (*30*)

shall not know what it is until tomorrow. (*38*)

15

I am sure it would be a good thing if (*10*)

we older ones could all get used to thinking in (*20*)

litres and metres, rather than in pints and yards but, (*30*)

of course, it is difficult to change the habits of (*40*)

a lifetime. (*42*)

16

A knowledge of reference books is essential to all typists (*10*)

if they wish to be able to give an answer (*20*)

to many queries. It is not a matter of what (*30*)

one knows, but whether one knows where to go to (*40*)

find information that is important. (*45*)

17

.... It was once the case that if people were well (*10*)

..*Uz*... qualified, they would have no difficulty in finding work, but (*20*)

.... this is certainly not so today. The financial situation is (*30*)

.... such that only a few of those looking for jobs (*40*)

....*&*... have any success in obtaining them. Perhaps we pay too (*50*)

...*}*.... much attention to training for work and not enough to (*60*)

..*&*..... learning how to make the best use of our leisure. (*70*)

8 The X Blends

I

(shorthand) An extremely luxurious Axminster carpet was bought for the [executive *(10)*

(shorthand) suite in the annexe. *(14)*

2

(shorthand) The mixer I bought in the January sale was exempt *(10)*

.... from tax, so it was not as expensive as I *(20)*

.... had expected it to be. *(25)*

3

(shorthand) We expect to receive the estimate for painting the exterior *(10)*

.... of the office block by the end of this week. *(20)*

4

(shorthand) Next week we shall make an excursion to the exhibition *(10)*

(shorthand) of French paintings. They are said to be extremely modern. *(20)*

5

(shorthand) After the executive had started up his own business, he *(10)*

(shorthand) had to engage a tax specialist to ensure accuracy in *(20)*

(shorthand) his accounts. *(22)*

6

(shorthand) As the government tax on the local spirits was so *(10)*

(shorthand) inexpensive, the exporter felt it would be worthwhile to expand *(20)*

.... the wholesale side of the business. *(26)*

7

The bank made extensive enquiries and, because of the [extremely (*10*)

special circumstances in this particular case, the mortgage was [extended (*20*)

for a maximum period of three years. (*27*)

8

A request from Rex for my expert opinion on the (*10*)

Saxon church gave me the excuse I had been looking (*20*)

for to exchange ideas and extend my knowledge of the (*30*)

old buildings in Exeter. (*34*)

9

Max bought an Axminster carpet from that exclusive store in (*10*)

Exmouth where we had tea the day we were on (*20*)

the excursion last October. He is delighted with his purchase, (*30*)

though he admits he has been extremely extravagant. (*38*)

10

We all tend to be extravagant at holiday times and (*10*)

New Year. It is extraordinary how much money disappears on (*20*)

gifts, food and drink during the festive season and once (*30*)

the old year is extinct, the January sales make extensive (*40*)

inroads into what remains in our pockets, purses and handbags. (*50*)

9   The N and V Blends

I

..꒦... Vera and Vernon vied with each other in every way   *(10)*

..ℰ,... but their behaviour was never vindictive.   *(16)*

2

..꒦ꞁ... Cheese and wine evenings are a modern innovation and much   *(10)*

.ᴄ꒦ᵖ... used nowadays as fund-raising events.   *(16)*

3

ℓ꒦..ꝉ. The scientist volunteered to have the new virus injected into   *(10)*

..꒦ᵇ.... his veins so that the doctors could evaluate the results   *(20)*

.ᴧᵉ-ᵇ... of their investigations.   *(23)*

4

..ℰ.... We shall be flying to Florida about the business partnership   *(10)*

...ᴧₓ₁. in November but intend to have a relaxing journey home   *(20)*

....ℰ.... by sea next February.   *(24)*

5

..ℰꞁ... When a bunch of vandals visited the town for the   *(10)*

..ᴼ�===.. football match, windows were smashed and violence shown to   *(20)*
    [anyone   *(20)*

.....✓.. who tried to interfere.   *(24)*

6

.ᴄᴜᵏ.. The invitations to the New Year's Eve dance were sent   *(10)*

.ꝉℰ.... out as a 'thank you' to everyone who had been   *(20)*

.ᴧℰ.... involved with the voluntary distribution of the newspaper.   *(28)*

7

.... Every Christmas Eve, the family were entertained by the
[children. (10)

...~~.. During the evening, songs were sung and verses recited, but (20)

...~... the best event that year, was a violin solo by (30)

.... Eva. (31)

8

..|2.√.. An old saying tells us that patience is a virtue (10)

...↓.... but obviously not possessed by everyone, because it goes on (20)

.... to say that it is seldom found in a woman (30)

.... and never in a man. (35)

9

.√..ƒ. The mass invasion of our seaside towns at bank holidays (10)

...↗.... by rival gangs of hooligans now seems to be accepted (20)

——.... as an annual event. The occasions are dreaded by local (30)

——.... traders, who think that they have got off very lightly (40)

.... if only a few of their shops have been the (50)

...↗.~. targets of vandals. (53)

10

.... The evening excursion turned out to be extremely exciting. A (10)

..↗.... fire that started in the coach was very soon extinguished, (20)

.6..... but then the driver was booked for exceeding the speed (30)

.√...↓.. limit near the Exchange. Finally, the vehicle narrowly missed a (40)

..↗.↗, bulldozer parked near to the excavations. Eventually, the
[excruciating experience (50)

.... ended and everyone except the children was glad of it. (60)

10   The C Blends

1

....*shorthand*.... Will you make sure that the tickets for tonight's concert (10)

....*shorthand*.... are sent to this address, as they cannot be collected. (20)

2

...*shorthand*.... We do not expect to encounter any difficulties in setting (10)

.... up a new company to deal with the foreign business. (20)

3

....*shorthand*.... Nowadays, much of the convenience food we buy contains
[chemical (10)

....*shorthand*.... substances, and the long-term effects of some of these (20)

....*shorthand*... additives are not known. (24)

4

....*shorthand*.... Close friendship is regarded by some as an unwelcome
[distraction. (10)

....*shorthand*.... They are unwilling to be totally committed to any other (20)

...*shorthand*.... person and like to keep their freedom. (27)

5

...*shorthand*.... The consumption of alcohol in this country is said to (10)

.... be rising. From all accounts, we are becoming a country (20)

...*shorthand*.... of wine and champagne drinkers, when we can afford it. (30)

6

...*shorthand*... Did you see the advertisement for the short course in (10)

_..⎤..._ computer training which the college of commerce is offering for (20)

..ᵈᵗᶜ... sixth-form students? I think Constance should consider taking

[it. (30)

7

_..ᵍ.·χ._ The report was not satisfactory because the worker was

[inexperienced (10)

_..⎤...._ rather than incompetent, but although he was not blamed, he (20)

_...,...._ still had to finish it before it could be accepted (30)

_........._ by the committee. (33)

8

_..✓....._ It will be inconvenient for the economics teacher to accompany (10)

_........._ the students on their trip, as he will be needed (20)

_ᴧᵧ⁻...._ to invigilate an examination which will have to be held (30)

_........._ on the same day. (34)

9

_..⎰....._ One of the important happenings of this century was the (10)

_........._ landing of the first astronauts on the moon, but today (20)

_...⌒✓._ we take such things as a matter of course and (30)

_..⎜√ᵗ..._ are not particularly concerned about them. (36)

10

_...✓....._ As it would not be convenient for us to move (10)

_...ᴸᵔ...._ at the moment, we have asked the builders for an (20)

_⌒⌒ᵖⁱ_ estimate for modernizing and extending our existing home.

[We expect (30)

_..ℰ⁻ᵧ..._ to have a consultation with them shortly. (37)

11

It is uneconomical to economize on good quality food, as (10)

poor nutrition can result in impaired health, and expensive
[convenience (20)

foods are not always the best. Some experts say that (30)

fruit in its fresh state has more food value than (40)

when it is cooked. (44)

12

The latest designs of the commercial fashion houses have
[always (10)

been based on some recent event. A royal wedding, the (20)

conquest of outer space, or the appearance on the pop (30)

scene of some new singer, are all sufficient to contradict (40)

what have formerly been considered to be the leading styles. (50)

13

I am confident that, if asked, the committee will be (10)

able to boost attendance at the lecture on Thursday. They (20)

cannot make it compulsory, but students will become interested
[if (30)

it is advertised that a famous actor will be making (40)

a contribution to it. I will ask them to compose (50)

a notice and get some posters ready. (57)

14

Dear Sir, Following the conversation we had on the telephone (10)

this morning, I enclose a draft of the contract for (20)

.... the consideration of your company. I hope you can agree (30)

.... to give us a licence to convey goods from your (40)

.... factories to selected ports and I shall expect to hear (50)

.... from you as soon as you have discussed the matter (60)

.... with your fellow directors. Yours faithfully. (66)

15

.... A conference will be held at the Commercial Centre in (10)

.... Canterbury this coming February for all those concerned
[about conservation (20)

.... in this country. During the course of the conference, a (30)

.... committee will be elected to start a campaign to consider (40)

.... constructive suggestions for keeping the countryside free from
[pollution and (50)

.... to hold regional competitions. We hope you will be able (60)

.... to attend and to make a contribution to the discussions. (70)

16

.... Dear Madam, We are in receipt of your cheque, which (10)

.... came this morning, in settlement of your account. Unfortunately,
[the (20)

.... cheque was dated 6 March last year so this will (30)

.... need to be amended and initialled by you before we (40)

.... are able to pass it for payment through our bank. (50)

.... I return the cheque to you herewith and shall be (60)

.... glad if you will return it to me, duly altered (70)

.... at your earliest convenience. Yours faithfully, for Sovereign
[Construction Company. (80)

II   The P Blends

I

..*shorthand*.. The new edition of the weekly educational supplement has been (*10*)

..*shorthand*.. launched in a blaze of publicity. (*16*)

2

..*shorthand*.. A permit must be applied for before entry to the (*10*)

..*shorthand*.. palace can be gained by the builders. (*17*)

3

..*shorthand*.. The waiter said he could recommend the plum and apple (*10*)

..*shorthand*.. tart, which was the chef's special for the day. (*19*)

4

..*shorthand*.. I think I am entitled to an explanation for the (*10*)

..*shorthand*.. reason why it has taken so much time to reply (*20*)

..*shorthand*.. to my complaint. (*23*)

5

..*shorthand*.. The application for planning permission is going ahead, but
[there (*10*)

..*shorthand*.. might be some slight delay before all the members of (*20*)

..*shorthand*.. the public concerned have been informed. (*26*)

6

..*shorthand*.. We plan to employ more people in order to publish (*10*)

..*shorthand*.. a colour supplement, but we must first consult the management (*20*)

..*shorthand*.. and explore the union's attitude to the idea. (*28*)

7

..⟨shorthand⟩.. Some people who are in full-time employment earn low (10)

..⟨shorthand⟩.. wages and are caught in the poverty trap, but do (20)

..⟨shorthand⟩.. not know that supplementary benefits can be applied for. (29)

Prepare for dictation:

8

..⟨shorthand⟩.. The weather was appalling throughout the whole fortnight of

[our (10)

..⟨shorthand⟩.. holiday, with rain splashing down every day, so all in (20)

..⟨shorthand⟩.. all, we were pleased to be home again. Strangely enough, (30)

..⟨shorthand⟩.. we decided to try the same resort the following year, (40)

..⟨shorthand⟩.. but this time the weather was splendid with ample sunshine. (50)

9

..⟨shorthand⟩.. Few people can accept unpleasant facts, especially if their

[acceptance (10)

..⟨shorthand⟩.. makes it necessary for them to alter their existing habits. (20)

..⟨shorthand⟩.. Only a few will make an effort to change their (30)

..⟨shorthand⟩.. plans even when they know that it will be more (40)

..⟨shorthand⟩.. rewarding in the long run for them to do so. (50)

10

..⟨shorthand⟩.. Dear Sir, I am pleased to inform you that the (10)

..⟨shorthand⟩.. sample templates about which you enquired early last week have (20)

..⟨shorthand⟩.. been supplied by our wholesalers and are now in stock. (30)

..⟨shorthand⟩.. They are being kept for you at the trade counter (40)

..⟨shorthand⟩.. and can be collected whenever it is convenient. Yours faithfully. (50)

11

Dear Mrs Temple, Thank you for your application form and (*10*)

remittance for tickets for the forthcoming concert to be given (*20*)

by the Pavilion Players. The response to date has been (*30*)

excellent and applications will be dealt with in strict rotation (*40*)

as soon as the booking plan is open. Yours sincerely. (*50*)

12

In reply to questions from members of the public, the (*10*)

explorer explained why the expedition had come about and how (*20*)

it had been planned. Getting the right people together was (*30*)

the first step and only a few of the many (*40*)

who had applied were accepted. Then there was the complicated (*50*)

task of buying in supplies and equipment for the journey. (*60*)

38

12   Simple Word Beginnings and Endings

I

(shorthand) This company will undertake to inspect your damaged carpet [and   (10)

(shorthand) repair it with invisible thread if it is within our   (20)

(shorthand) capabilities.   (21)

2

(shorthand) There is a distinct possibility that three coats of undercoat   (10)

(shorthand) will be needed to give sufficient coverage over the dark   (20)

(shorthand) paint underneath.   (22)

3

(shorthand) It is the responsibility of all typists to check the   (10)

(shorthand) work that they undertake for any spelling errors, transpositions [or   (20)

(shorthand) any other mistakes.   (23)

4

(shorthand) Some cars are now fitted with transverse engines and one   (10)

(shorthand) advantage is that the various movable parts are more easily   (20)

(shorthand) accessible when servicing.   (23)

5

(shorthand) It transpired that the leading lady had gastric trouble so   (10)

(shorthand) the understudy overcame her nervousness and played the part at (20)

(shorthand) very short notice.   (23)

6

..6ₑₘ I asked the bank manager about the possibility of an (10)

..⌣ⱼ.. overdraft, but it transpired that there is not much cash (20)

..⌐ᵔ... available at the moment. (24)

7

⁊ⱽ ·ⱽ⁻ We require the machinery to be overhauled as soon as (10)

.... possible, so will you please let us have your estimate (20)

.... before the end of the week. (26)

8

.ɓ...... The insurance company said that the difficulties in transporting
[the (10)

ᴏ∧.⌸ sable coat could be overcome if it was packed securely (20)

ᴜⱼ.Ⳑₐ in a strong box, insured and adequately labelled. (28)

Prepare for dictation:

9

.ɓ⁻.... Dear Householder, We are specialists in roofing work who
[undertake (10)

⁊....ɣ.. repairs to slates, tiles, gables, eaves and guttering – in fact, (20)

⁻⁻⁻⁻⁻ all the places overhead where the amateur cannot reach without (30)

.... safe and suitable ladders and equipment. Simply give us a (40)

.... ring when you have a few minutes available using the (50)

⌀ℓ.... Freefone number at the head of this letter. Yours faithfully. (60)

10

.... Many overseas students, who come to this country from all (10)

..*...* over the world to advance their studies, are supported by (20)

..*...* loans from their respective governments which they undertake to
[repay (30)

..*...* when they return home again. During training, their academic
[ability (40)

..*...*is sometimes underestimated when really it is difficulty in
[translating (50)

..*...* the English language which is the root of the trouble. (60)

13   The R Principle

1

I bought my brother a brand-new power tool for   (10)

Christmas and he gave me a bright brass carving of   (20)

a blackbird.   (22)

2

I enjoy doing puzzles with cryptic clues but must admit   (10)

that, despite great mental effort, I am rarely able to   (20)

complete them.   (22)

3

The brandy glass was gradually filled to the brim so   (10)

that an exact estimate of its capacity could be agreed   (20)

upon by the organizers of the competition.   (27)

4

The order for the brake linings must be treated as   (10)

urgent, and must be dealt with immediately, even though we (20)

are in arrears with all our deliveries.   (27)

5

Householders are constantly being criticized by the fire
[brigade for (10)

failing to be aware of the dangers of using chip   (20)

pans, which are often burning briskly before being discovered. (29)

6

When the grim news that the car had crashed was   (10)

... ⌒ ... brought to the girl, the cream jug she was holding (20)

... ⟋ .... slipped from her grasp and broke into small pieces. (29)

7

.. ⟋ ... The gratings under the bridge appear to be blocked with (10)

.... ⟋ ... grit and leaves, and this is causing much surface water (20)

... ⟋ .... to lie across the roadway, thus creating a traffic hazard. (30)

8

. ⟋ ..... The boys in the next garden had arranged a game (10)

... ⟋ .... of cricket, so I am almost certain this was how (20)

.. ⟋ ..... the greenhouse window became cracked, but no one would admit (30)

...... ⟋ . to being responsible for the breakage. (36)

9

. ⟋ In our view, it would be a good thing to (10)

. ⟋ .. invest more money in the railways, and if fares were (20)

.... reduced, more of us would travel by train instead of (30)

.... by car and coach. This would take a lot of (40)

. ⟋ . traffic off roads which are already too crowded. (48)

10

.. ⟋ ..... The cross-country runners had a gruelling time last weekend (10)

.... ⟋ ... in appalling weather conditions. They were eventually reduced to

                   [creeping (20)

.. ⟋ .... and crawling through the mud on the last lap and (30)

. ⟋ .... the champion, who had taken the lead from the beginning (40)

...... ⟋ was forced to withdraw with cramp in his leg muscles. (50)

14　The PR Series of Word Beginnings

1

...｜o✓... Preparatory to making arrangements to defend the prisoner, I

[would　(10)

｜↙.6ᵖ' appreciate preliminary briefing about his background.　(16)

2

..｜↙..... All types of pressure groups seem to be in the　(10)

｜↙⌐.6ᴎ news nowadays, persistently protesting about one cause or

[another.　(19)

3

.ٱ˺ᴄ.... The most successful apprentice of the year, to mark his　(10)

....ˇ.... achievement in the workshop, was presented with items of

[electrical　(20)

.... equipment by the Chairman.　(24)

4

...｜˹ᴢ... It is not practical for me to collect my order　(10)

...｜v.ᴾᵇ.. today as I promised. Can you bring my provisions when　(20)

..ᴎ⌒⌐.. you collect your own?　(24)

5

⌐⌐⌐ᴖᵧ. The news of the merger left some of the shareholders　(10)

..↰⌐... feeling apprehensive, so they decided it was important to express (20)

..⌐⌐ᴑᴎ⌒their disagreement in writing to the Board.　(27)

6

.⌐ᵗᴑ⌐.... I am a little apprehensive about the protest meeting to　(10)

express disapproval about Parliament's latest attempt to limit
profits. We (20)

must be prepared for a long and noisy session in (30)

the House. (32)

7

It is important that your representatives make a good impression (10)

on those with whom they propose to do business, and (20)

experience will show them how to make the right approach (30)

to difficult customers. (33)

8

It is highly improbable that such a prominent social figure (10)

is in the employ of a foreign government, but the (20)

situation is so delicate that the matter has been referred (30)

to the Prime Minister. (34)

9

Some people will do almost anything, however reprehensible, to
[get (10)

publicity, and as newspapers are prepared to publish rumours of (20)

romances, which they know will please members of the public, (30)

it is not difficult to realize this ambition to become (40)

news. (41)

Prepare for dictation:

10

From time to time, there are world shortages of various (10)

commodities, such as grain, coffee and cocoa. Sometimes these
[are (20)

due to bad harvests, sometimes to economic factors and
[sometimes (30)

because of war or natural disasters like a flood. A (40)

.... bad grain harvest will push up the price of bread. (50)

A shortage of feeding stuffs will bring about a rise (60)

in the cost of meat or milk. Late frosts in (70)

the spring can cause a shortage of summer fruit, and (80)

.... long, hot, dry spells can result in a shortage of (90)

root crops. (92)

I5 General Review Exercises (2)

Put into Teeline and then type or read back:

I

... The company will discontinue trading because of the publicity
[recently (*10*)

... given to its inability to pay its debts. (*18*)

2

... I think we should all welcome an exchange of views (*10*)

... on the contents of this communiqué before we issue a (*20*)

... public statement. (*22*)

3

... Now that we are thinking of engaging extra staff, I (*10*)

... suggest we should advertise immediately for someone who
[speaks a (*20*)

... foreign language fluently. (*23*)

4

... It is strange how members within a community can be (*10*)

... drawn closer together as soon as there is any real (*20*)

... trouble facing them, yet be divided at other times. (*29*)

5

... We expect the next examination to be held in November, (*10*)

... but we will give you the maximum amount of notice (*20*)

... about the exact date. (*24*)

6

If you complete and return the enclosed form at your (10)

earliest convenience, you can expect to hear something to your (20)

advantage in the immediate future. (25)

7

A decision was taken by the committee to expel one (10)

of its members when it became known that he had (20)

become involved in illegal dealings. (25)

8

Many recent strikes have caused inconvenience to members of
[the (10)

public who cannot do anything to help settle the disputes (20)

and who simply have to suffer over and over again. (30)

9

However inconvenient it may be for you to attend the (10)

meeting, it would, nevertheless, enable us to find out at (20)

first hand what their attitude is to this commercial venture. (30)

10

The further we went down the valley, the less clearly (10)

could we see our way, as the existing tracks were (20)

covered by vegetation, so we decided to go no further (30)

but to retrace our steps before we became utterly exhausted. (40)

Prepare for dictation:

11

The Chairman said the accounts showed a drop in profits (10)

from those of the previous year. The Yorkshire branches were (20)

doing much better at present than those in other parts (30)

of the country. He and the Board regretted that they (40)

could not recommend the usual annual dividend to be paid. (50)

12

The new book *Cooking for Pleasure*, just published, contains [clear (10)

instructions for people with little or no cooking experience and (20)

explains how, with a mixture of pluck and ambition, and (30)

the right ingredients, the beginner can produce meals to please. (40)

Plenty of simple menus are given, which are both easy (50)

to prepare and economical to produce. It is indeed a (60)

bumper cookery book with nothing essential to the learner [omitted. (70)

13

Dear Sir, I am in possession of your recent publicity (10)

material and advertisements, but I am sorry to say that (20)

I appear to have lost the tear-off slip inviting (30)

members of the public to make application for your *Mammoth* (40)

Dictionary for examination in their own homes. I expect to (50)

be able to make maximum use of this dictionary in (60)

.... connection with my work as a commercial representative, so if   (70)

.... it is not putting you to any inconvenience, I shall   (80)

.... be glad if you will send me a copy as   (90)

.... soon as possible, enclosing your account for the book and   (100)

.... anything extra you may charge for postage and packing. Yours   (110)

.... faithfully.   (111)

16 Word Beginnings

1

..... A translator will be available for the transmission of the (*10*)

programmes to the under-privileged countries. (*16*)

2

Semiquavers are short musical notes. Sixteen of them are needed (*10*)

to make up a semibreve. (*15*)

3

The electrician sent by the Electricity Board did a magnificent (*10*)

repair job on the central-heating system. (*17*)

4

When people undergo heart transplants, it is the after-effects (*10*)

that cause anxiety, rather than the actual operation. (*18*)

5

It transpired that the ex-pilot lived in a new (*10*)

self-contained flat near to the aerodrome underpass. (*18*)

6

From what was said after the post-mortem, we understand (*10*)

the use of these aerosols will be banned hereafter in (*20*)

airless places. (*22*)

7

Magnolia trees appear in all their magnificence about Easter

[time (*10*)

..... and it seems such a pity that the blossom has (20)

..... to fade and cannot be everlasting. (26)

8

..... Some people regard belief in the supernatural as simple
[superstition (10)

..... and nonsense while others study the subject in depth and (20)

..... are quite certain as to its authenticity. (27)

9

..... The question was whether the sailor, overcome by the semi- (10)

..... tropical heat, had fallen overboard, or whether he had been (20)

..... overpowered in the semi-darkness and thrown over the side. (30)

10

..... A multiplicity of household goods are electroplated. That is,
[they (10)

..... are coated with silver by a process of electrolysis, which (20)

..... makes them cheaper than if they were made wholly of (30)

..... silver. (31)

11

..... Some people do not like wearing jewellery made with semi- (10)

..... precious stones. Certainly there is nothing to equal the
[magnificence (20)

..... of diamonds, but the everlasting charm of a well-set (30)

..... and polished agate or opal is often under-estimated. (39)

17 Word Endings

1

.... Parapsychology is a relatively new science. It is concerned with (*10*)

.... the study of strange occurrences like telepathy. (*17*)

2

.... Archaeologists need to know something about biology and [sociology in (*10*)

.... order to piece together the fragments they dig up when (*20*)

.... excavating old settlements. (*23*)

3

.... Fidelity and humility are old-fashioned qualities that seem to (*10*)

.... have little place today in a world full of artificial (*20*)

.... standards and superficial show. (*24*)

4

.... I should not care myself to live in an apartment (*10*)

.... near the experimental research establishment. The element of risk [would (*20*)

.... be a worry to me. (*25*)

5

.... Because of the fog, visibility was so poor that the (*10*)

.... broken overhead cable was invisible to the driver and he (*20*)

.... was unable to avoid being hit by it as it (*30*)

.... bounced in his direction. (*34*)

6

.... Some people wear clothes because they are fashionable, even if (10)

.... they are not suitable or sensible but, being small, I (20)

.... have to wear what is available in my size and (30)

...~~_____~~hope I still look reasonably well-dressed. (37)

7

...~~...~~ The official complained that the outbreak of racial violence had (10)

.... not been reported in a responsible manner. The facts given (20)

...~~/s~~... were only partially correct. The problems of living in a (30)

...~~/s~~. multi-racial society had to be handled carefully and patiently (40)

...~~...~~... if they were to be solved. (46)

8

...~~...~~. Anthropology is the study of humans and their customs, which (10)

~~...~~means taking into account their physiological and psychological
[reactions at (20)

~~...~~all stages of development. Anthropologists often live with the
[tribes (30)

.... they are studying for several years to get as complete (40)

.... a picture of them, as possible. (46)

9

...~~...~~... Graphology is the art of reading a person's character from (10)

...~~...~~ study of handwriting. Some firms employ the services of (20)

...~~...~~. a graphologist to help in deciding which candidate will be (30)

...~~...~~.. best fitted to fill a vacancy. Others arrange for prospective (40)

54

.... employees to be interviewed by a psychologist, so that any　(50)

.... temperamental abnormalities may be disclosed before an

[appointment is made.　(60)

Prepare for dictation:

10

.... Last night's documentary programme on television showed some of

[the　(10)

.... experimental work being done by biologists, psychologists and

[meteorologists. The　(20)

.... latter, of course, depend upon the reliability of their instruments (30)

.... in making assessments. I think that mental health is a　(40)

.... field in which much progress has been made in recent　(50)

.... years, mainly because it would not have been possible to　(60)

.... discuss mental illness openly in the past. Also, many other　(70)

.... illnesses have been found to have their roots in temperamental　(80)

.... disorders.　(81)

11

.... I could not make up my mind whether to buy　(10)

.... a television set or a music centre with the money　(20)

.... I had won in the nationwide crossword competition. After the　(30)

.... initial excitement had subsided, I asked myself which would be　(40)

.... the best investment for the future. It was so difficult　(50)

.... to make a decision that I finally compromised by hiring　(60)

.... a television and buying a music centre. The trouble is　(70)

55

.... that with paying the monthly instalments on the television and (80)

.... buying records I am now worse off than I was (90)

.... before I won the contest! (95)

12

.... Dear Sir, We should like to draw your attention to (10)

.... the commercially desirable property which is being offered for
[sale (20)

.... shortly by auction. With some financial assistance, which we can (30)

.... arrange for you, and a few well-planned alterations, it (40)

.... would be possible to transform this delightful mansion into a (50)

.... fashionable hotel. The entrance, for instance, is especially suitable
[for (60)

.... that purpose and the grounds provide ample space for any (70)

.... necessary extensions. You would be well advised to let us (80)

.... know at once if you desire to purchase, as we (90)

.... shall be unable to hold it for you unless we (100)

.... know you are definitely interested. Yours faithfully. (107)

18   General Review Exercises (3)

Put into Teeline and read or type back:

1

.|乚....   In certain circumstances, pre-fabricated buildings provide a very

                                                                       [satisfactory   (*10*)

....   alternative to traditional ones.   (*14*)

2

...ク....   The object of education should be to prepare people for   (*10*)

....   life and not just to train them for work.   (*19*)

3

...ﾉ.ゎ.   Few people like having injections and would prefer to take   (*10*)

乙...-ଌ   pills to combat disease if they had the choice.   (*19*)

4

....   Many prominent sportsmen and sportswomen and pop stars

                                                       [become multi-   (*10*)

  millionaires once they have established their superiority over

                                                       others in   (*20*)

....   their respective fields.   (*23*)

5

..o—⌐..   Semi-detached houses are generally cheaper than those standing

                                                            [alone,   (*10*)

..ﾞ......   but detached houses in the north of England are cheaper   (*20*)

......ゎ..   than semi-detached houses in the south of the country.   (*30*)

6

...ﾞ....   As a nation, we depend upon our agricultural industry to   (*10*)

..*S*..... keep the supermarket shelves full, but it is still necessary   (*20*)

.... to bring in many items of food that are impossible   (*30*)

..*?*..... to grow here.   (*33*)

Prepare for speed-building drill:

7

..*P*... Perhaps most of us believe in some superstitions, but probably   (*10*)

..*IV*.... not all of us would be prepared to admit it.   (*20*)

8

.... The house was perfectly situated on the shores of a   (*10*)

.... lake with superb views of the mountains which surrounded it.   (*20*)

9

..*Vh*.... The principal said that the school had been established in   (*10*)

..*C18*.... the eighteenth century to enable the sons of merchants to   (*20*)

...*?*..... receive a good general education.   (*25*)

10

..*Gh*... In a comprehensive statement, the archbishop's representative
                                      [said it was   (*10*)

..*cG*... important to move slowly and carefully if their proposals were   (*20*)

..*1*..... not to be rejected by the other side.   (*28*)

11

..*jv*.... The Prime Minister said that a preliminary meeting with the   (*10*)

..*La*.... heads of state would be held as soon as an   (*20*)

...*1L*.... appropriate time and place had been agreed between them.   (*29*)

12

... *shorthand* ... A proportion of the committee was prepared to give its   *(10)*

... *shorthand* ... approval to the proposal, but approximately half objected to it,   *(20)*

... *shorthand* ... so it was decided to discuss the subject again at   *(30)*

... *shorthand* ... the next meeting before taking a final vote.   *(38)*

19   Special and Reduced Outlines

The following exercises include many of the words to be found in the lists of special and reduced outlines at the end of *Teeline Revised Edition*. They can be put into Teeline or taken from dictation and checked by reading back, typing or transcribing into longhand, and can then be used for speed-building drill. *Remember* that although the use of reduced outlines helps to increase speed, words may be written more fully, if this is preferred.

I

.....*⟨outline⟩*..... It will be necessary for us to exchange frequent communiqués   (*10*)

.... if we are to get a full picture of the   (*20*)

.... subjects under discussion.   (*23*)

2

.... It is extraordinary that a man with so little experience   (*10*)

.... should be put in charge of an international organization without (*20*)

...*⟨outline⟩*... any consultation with the departments concerned.   (*26*)

3

..*⟨outline⟩*.... I do not think either of the main political parties   (*10*)

...*⟨outline⟩*... has sufficient influence today to form a really strong government (*20*)

..*⟨outline⟩*. without the support of minority groups.   (*26*)

4

..*⟨outline⟩*.... In the absence of the Chairman, who was attending an   (*10*)

.*⟨outline⟩*.. international conference in America, one of the ordinary members
                                                                   [presided (*20*)

.... at the meeting of the commercial society.   (*27*)

5

....✎.... We recently sent a comprehensive report on the electricity
[exhibition   (10)

✐.✑. to headquarters and, subsequently, were congratulated by the
[superintendent on   (20)

.... our detailed description of some of the equipment.
(28)

6

..✎.✎. Because of the amalgamation of our company with your
[organization,   (10)

..✎✎.. it is probable that there will be an improvement in
(20)

...✎✎.. the employment situation in this area next year.
(28)

7

...✎..... Have you seen the advertisement in the agency window about
(10)

...✎✎ the competition for an original design to go on National
(20)

..✎✎... Savings stamps? The closing date is Tuesday 20th February.
(29)

8

...✎✎. The Chairman said that although the majority of manufacturers
[would   (10)

✎....✎ like to instal the new machinery, many did not have
(20)

✎...✎ the necessary capital to take advantage of this technical
[development.   (30)

9

.... It is of the utmost importance that we have an
(10)

.... immediate enquiry into the finances of this firm. Please prepare
(20)

.....✎... a report on their turnover and profits for the past
(30)

.... two years.
(32)

10

... **♪** .... It is said that opportunity knocks but once, so it (*10*)

... **✍** ... would be wise not to ignore any opportunity which presents (*20*)

... **✍** ..... itself; otherwise, one might for ever regret not having taken (*30*)

. **⌐ŋ** ... advantage of it. (*33*)

11

... **✓ ⌐ŋ** ... On whose authority has the preliminary investigation into these [charges (*10*)

⌐ŋ
.... against the running of the institution been begun? Generally, [one (*20*)

.... can expect to be informed before such an exercise is (*30*)

.... set in motion. (*33*)

12

✦ ... **Ψ** ... They say the diplomat will be going to Europe to (*10*)

.... study agriculture in the Community countries, but no details of (*20*)

.... the visit have yet been made public, nor has any (*30*)

.... date been given for it. (*35*)

13

.... May we draw your attention to the fact that the (*10*)

.. **ſ** ..... enclosed reference urgently requires your signature, and the [delay is (*20*)

.. **Ⴚ** ..... causing much inconvenience to the employee concerned? Will you [please (*30*)

. **⌐ŋ** ... give the matter your immediate attention? (*36*)

14

... **⌐ŋ** .. Notwithstanding a drop in profits for the year ending last (*10*)

.... November, I think we can say that the business generally (20)

.... is in a satisfactory state, taking into account the state (30)

....𝒴.... of the nation as a whole. (36)

Suggested groupings: ....ᶻᶜ... taking into account

.... ᶻᶜ taking account (of)

15

.... In principle, we are in favour of population control, but (10)

...𝑉/... we do not think this subject should be given priority (20)

.... at the discussion, as we prefer to spend the maximum (30)

.... amount of time on other important matters. (37)

16

⌒𝓎...⌐ I think the magistrate showed prejudice in his judgement of (10)

...𝓎ᶜᶜ. the accident case. All the circumstances pointed to negligence

[on (20)

...𝓎..... the part of the authority, but he ignored several significant (30)

..𝓸𝓎ᶜ.. pieces of evidence in his summing up. (37)

17

⌒⌒⌒ Will you please prepare a memorandum to enclose with the (10)

⌒𝓎..�6. magazine, reminding all members of the association that their

[subscriptions (20)

———ᴌ̵ are due at the end of this month, and drawing (30)

...ᶻ... their attention to the increased charges for delivery? (38)

18

.... We should like to receive from you samples of the (10)

.⌒𝓎ᴌ.. imported cloth you mentioned when we last spoke on the (20) telephone, together with details of the price and the minimum (*30*)

quantity you would be prepared to sell us. (*38*)

19

I must congratulate you on the prompt attention given to (*10*)

our recent orders and on the high quality of the (*20*)

goods received. If these standards can be maintained, we are (*30*)

prepared to place further substantial orders in the near future. (*40*)

20

An examination of all our English establishments showed that in (*10*)

the north, production was approximately ten per cent higher

[than (*20*)

in the south. It is difficult to say why this (*30*)

should be so, but an enquiry may throw some light (*40*)

upon the matter. (*43*)

21

I have given much thought to the scheme you have (*10*)

prepared for us, but there are a few questions I (*20*)

should like to ask you before deciding whether or not (*30*)

we should adopt it. Will you telephone me at this (*40*)

department so that we can arrange a meeting? (*48*)

22

It was inevitable that, sooner or later, the government would (*10*)

require information on the administration of this organization

[and, in (*20*)

64

particular, the source of its income. It is remarkable that (30)

things have been allowed to go on as they have (40)

done already without such an enquiry taking place. (48)

23

Taking into account all the circumstances and the amount of (10)

time still available to us, I think we should bring (20)

the matter to the attention of the relevant government
[department (30)

immediately, so that any action that is considered to be (40)

necessary can be taken before it is too late. (49)

24

Nothing has been heard for several months from my old (10)

acquaintance who was sent by his insurance firm to the (20)

U.S.A. I used to get regular letters from (30)

him, giving interesting descriptions of life over there, but now (40)

all communication has ceased. I do hope nothing serious has (50)

happened to him. (53)

25

Illness may be a reaction to chemicals in food, to (10)

which some people are allergic. Colour is often added to (20)

food to make it look more attractive, for example, orange (30)

to drinks and green to tinned peas. Even bread may (40)

contain a preservative to make sure it does not go (50)

mouldy on the supermarket shelves. Both tea and coffee contain (60)

65

.... a drug which can cause illness in some people. Statements   (70)

...𝒵..... about allergies have been challenged by food analysts, who say   (80)

.... food preservatives and chemicals are safe. While they will not   (90)

.... actually poison us, some people are especially sensitive to them. (100)

...β..... If you suspect that you suffer from a food allergy,   (110)

.... it is suggested that you eat only fresh meat or   (120)

...ℓ..... fish, fresh fruit and vegetables and drink only spa water   (130)

.... to see if the illness goes. Then, processed foods should   (140)

.... be introduced into the diet one at a time to   (150)

.... see which bring back the symptoms. There are a few   (160)

.... doctors who specialize in treating food allergies, but many who (170)

.... think the whole idea is nonsense.   (176)

20   Ten Twenty-Word Passages for Speed Building

I

.... From our information it seems to be true that the   (10)

...~~.... inspectors have threatened to resign unless working conditions

[are investigated. (20)

2

.... After a careful examination of the note, the expert came   (10)

.... to the conclusion that it was an extremely clever forgery.   (20)

3

.... The fact that you have completed the tests, has enabled   (10)

.... me to make a full assessment of your experimental work.   (20)

4

.... Special arrangements have been made to hold the social evening (10)

.... at the town hall and we hope you will come.   (20)

5

.... People in the academic world sometimes assume that those with (10)

.... technical qualifications have less ability than those with book

[learning. (20)

6

.... The party should include a biologist, a photographer, a doctor   (10)

.... and someone who understands the language to act as interpreter. (20)

7

.... It is possible that a transfer of income from the   (10)

.... company to ourselves would lead to an involved tax situation.   (20)

8

Considering she was responsible for their difficulties, I have no *(10)*

hesitation in condemning her selfish action in refusing them

[accommodation. *(20)*

9

If we intend to inspect the property this afternoon, we *(10)*

must leave early, as it is an hour's drive away. *(20)*

10

Provided they can arrange a better distribution of the goods, *(10)*

we can promise them increased profits in the coming year. *(20)*

21   General Dictation Passages

1

...〳... In this day and age, most women in business expect   (*10*)

.... to get equal pay with their male colleagues, but many   (*20*)

.... point out that they still do not get equal opportunities   (*30*)

.... for promotion.   (*32*)

2

.... Dear Sir, Thank you for your letter with cheque enclosed   (*10*)

.... which arrived yesterday. We are pleased to know that you   (*20*)

.... were completely satisfied with the last delivery of goods and (*30*)

...┬─ๅ... we shall give prompt attention to your present order. We   (*40*)

.... expect to dispatch it some time next week. Yours faithfully.   (*50*)

3

...〆〕... Ladies and Gentlemen, It is my pleasant duty as Chairman   (*10*)

...〵... of your Board to tell you that our profits today   (*20*)

.... are higher than they have ever been in the history   (*30*)

...〳... of the company. In spite of heavy expenditure on plant   (*40*)

...〵... and machinery, we can still declare a final dividend which   (*50*)

...〵... is better than last year's.   (*55*)

4

...〵... I have rarely encountered such an accomplished performer on

                                                              [such   (*10*)

...〵... a variety of instruments, but I felt it was inconsiderate   (*20*) of the audience to expect more than one encore. However (30)

encouraging their enthusiasm, the artist must have been
[exhausted and (40)

they should have allowed him to retire from the stage (50)

when he had finished his act. (56)

5

If you ever have any additional news, it would be (10)

a good idea to telephone the manager. The best time (20)

would be before the business meeting, but to make sure (30)

that the external telephone lines are not engaged I would (40)

suggest ringing first thing in the morning. At that time (50)

one can be almost certain that the lines are free. (60)

6

The completion of income tax forms worries many people and (10)

they cannot understand how their coding numbers are worked
[out (20)

or the grounds on which they can object. However, as (30)

some mistakes in these assessments are inevitable, it is in (40)

one's own interests to give proper attention to the problem (50)

and to study the explanatory leaflets which are usually enclosed. (60)

7

The taking of drugs cannot solve our problems, but can (10)

only multiply them. The initial effect of a drug may (20)

be to induce an elated mood as reality fades and (30)

.... the memory grows dim. But, as the effect wears off, (*40*)

..✗...... we are forced to return to a greyer world, much (*50*)

.... less able to cope with life than we were before. (*60*)

8

.... The speaker said that future prospects were grim. We could (*10*)

.... expect a further rise in unemployment and a smaller share (*20*)

..✐....... of the export market trade. Those on fixed incomes would (*30*)

.... find they were unable to meet the increased costs that (*40*)

.... would have to be paid. At last people realized that (*50*)

.... there had to be a change in attitudes if the (*60*)

.... situation was to be improved. (*65*)

9

...⎧⎧___Dear Sir, Thank you for your order, which we have (*10*)

.... received today, for one dozen rose bushes. These will be (*20*)

.... dispatched to you by rail as soon as possible and (*30*)

.... should be delivered to you before the end of the (*40*)

..⎰⎰..... month. We enclose our new price list which operates from (*50*)

.... 1st November. May we assure you of our prompt attention (*60*)

.... at all times. Yours faithfully. (*65*)

10

..∫...... Dear Madam, Further to our telephone conversation of
[yesterday, I (*10*)

..⸰....... now have pleasure in informing you that we are sending (*20*)

⌣⌣ℓ⸰ you, under separate cover, a replacement for the damaged tea (*30*)

71

.... service which you returned to us last week. We hope (*40*)

.... this will reach you in good condition and that you (*50*)

.... will have no further cause for complaint. We greatly regret (*60*)

.... any inconvenience caused. Yours faithfully. (*65*)

11

.... The recent rise in unemployment is causing much concern to (*10*)

.... leaders of trade and industry, who say the standard of (*20*)

.... living of their members is falling lower and lower. They (*30*)

.... blame the economic policy being pursued by the present
[government. (*40*)

.... Hour by hour and day by day, the situation seems (*50*)

.... to be deteriorating. Some form of wages freeze must be (*60*)

.... agreed if prices are not to rise higher and higher (*70*)

.... as the months pass. (*74*)

12

.... If you want to increase the number of words a (*10*)

.... minute you can write in Teeline in the days to (*20*)

.... come, you should try to set aside so many hours (*30*)

.... a week for regular practice. Half an hour a day (*40*)

.... is a reasonable amount of time, although it is better (*50*)

.... to study for only a quarter of an hour every (*60*)

.... day than to do an hour and three quarters only (*70*)

.... twice a week, or several hours only once a week. (*80*)

13

.... When one learns a skill, it is the amount of (10)

.... regular practice that determines how good one becomes, not how (20)

.⌣̅⌒̅ᄀ.. well one understands the principles underlying it. History

[students learn (30)

.... certain facts and are considered good if they can remember (40)

.... and reproduce those facts in answer to questions. There is (50)

.... time for them to plan their answers and to think (60)

.... carefully before writing them down. The student of a skill (70)

..⅋.... is in no such happy position. It is useless knowing (80)

.... what notes to strike in playing a piece of music (90)

.... if the fingers are not trained by sufficient practice to (100)

.... hit the notes correctly and immediately. The examiner does not (110)

.... want to wait while the student thinks what to do (120)

.... next. Shorthand students are in a similar position. They cannot (130)

.... stop to plan what must be written when taking down (140)

.... a passage from dictation and this is where the immediate (150)

..ᖇ.... and spontaneous recall of outlines through much practice

[pays off. (160)

22 Ten 100-Word Passages for Speed Building

I

When a girl decides she wants to be a secretary (*10*)

she does not always know exactly what she is undertaking. (*20*)

Perhaps she imagines herself as the 'right hand' of some (*30*)

busy important person of business, and thinks of travelling with (*40*)

them about Europe or America, checking their time-table and (*50*)

arranging for their accommodation, making sure that they are
[not (*60*)

troubled by callers for whom their personal attention is not (*70*)

necessary. Often she does not think of the long training (*80*)

and hard study which must come first, or of the (*90*)

not very interesting days of office routine and repetitive jobs. (*100*)

2

Dear Madam, Thank you for your letter of yesterday, and (*10*)

for your offer to assist in our scheme to provide (*20*)

a cheap and efficient cleaning service for offices and homes. (*30*)

We expect that most of the work we shall require (*40*)

from our employees will be of a fairly light character. (*50*)

The small amount of heavy work, when it does occur, (*60*)

will be given to our present staff, who are used (*70*)

to moving large pieces of furniture, cleaning outside windows,
[etc. (*80*)

.... If you are interested in joining our team of workers, (*90*)

.... please call, or telephone me, during office hours. Yours
[faithfully. (*100*)

3

.... Dear Madam, We very much regret having to draw attention (*10*)

.... to the fact that payment of your account is now (*20*)

.... two months overdue. A month ago, we sent you a (*30*)

ᵃ⁊ .... statement of account, bearing a reminder slip, assuming that the (*40*)

⌒⌒ account had merely escaped your notice and that we should (*50*)

⌒ᶜ have your remittance within a few days. It now appears (*60*)

⌒⊤ that we were mistaken and, unless we receive the amount (*70*)

34|₆82 outstanding, that is thirty-four pounds, eighty-two pence, within (*80*)

.... the next four days, we shall be obliged to take (*90*)

ᵃᵉℓ action distasteful to us and embarrassing to yourself. Yours
[faithfully. (*100*)

4

ᶻᵉ ⁊⊢ Dear Sirs, I was shocked and rather annoyed to receive (*10*)

ʠ your letter of yesterday about an alleged overdue account. The (*20*)

.... amount you mention appears to refer to the purchase of (*30*)

ᵉ⌒ ᵉ∕ a suede skirt during your January sale. I was served (*40*)

.... by Miss Long, who knows me quite well, and on (*50*)

.... this occasion, I paid cash for my purchase instead of (*60*)

⊂⊇⊃ using my credit account. You must be aware that it (*70*)

.... has never been my custom to leave an account outstanding (*80*)

.... after each month end. Fortunately, I have kept the receipt (*90*)

.... and would like your explanation of the error. Yours faithfully. (*100*)

5

.... Dear Mrs Thurston, Thank you for your letter of 5th (*10*)

.... May. I am truly sorry that you have been caused (*20*)

.... annoyance by a very unusual error in our accounting system. (*30*)

.... It appears that Miss Long was called away while serving (*40*)

.... you, and when she returned you had paid another assistant (*50*)

.... for the skirt. Miss Long booked the purchase against your (*60*)

.... account, as you do not generally pay cash, and she (*70*)

.... assumed you had not done so on this occasion. I (*80*)

.... hope you can accept our explanation and not allow this (*90*)

.... unfortunate error to spoil the goodwill hitherto enjoyed. Yours
[sincerely. (*100*)

6

.... What do we mean when we talk about capital? Many (*10*)

.... people immediately think of money, but money is not the (*20*)

.... only form which capital takes. If you go into business (*30*)

.... by starting a shop, the capital used will take the (*40*)

.... form of stock, fixtures and fittings as well as cash (*50*)

.... for the many necessary payments. Your premises, shop fittings,
[etc. (*60*)

.... are known as fixed capital. Fixed capital goods are not (*70*)

.... sold, but are used continuously without much change. Current
[capital (*80*)

76

.... consists of cash and goods which can be sold for (90)

.... cash. Money for wages, etc., is commonly called liquid capital. (100)

7

.... In business, the word 'turnover' means the total sales made (10)

.... over a given period. This is generally expressed as a (20)

.... money amount. Thus, the annual turnover of a business is (30)

.... the money value of its sales during a year. Some (40)

.... businesses, such as retail shops, are expected to have a (50)

.... rapid stock turnover. That is, the average stock of goods (60)

.... is sold and replaced many times during a year. If (70)

.... the stock is one thousand pounds in value and it (80)

.... is turned over once a month, it has the effect (90)

.... of using twelve thousand pounds of capital in each year. (100)

8

.... Many a time I have heard people complain they are (10)

.... alone all day long and that hour after hour they (20)

.... have nothing to do. It is a good idea to (30)

.... make a plan for every day, having some definite aim (40)

.... for each part of it, even if it is only (50)

.... a walk to the shops for half an hour in (60)

.... the morning and a radio or television programme to fill (70)

.... in the evening. There is nothing worse than having time (80)

.... on one's hands, but with a little planning, one could (90)

.... make the most of enjoying it, instead of being bored. (100)

9

The hedgehog is one of the oldest types of mammal (*10*)

in existence. From about November until spring, hedgehogs

[hibernate. This (*20*)

long, sleeping fast renders them almost lifeless. They are useful (*30*)

animals in the garden as they will destroy slugs, snails (*40*)

and mice. They enjoy a saucer of milk, but will (*50*)

not usually drink from it in the daylight. When a (*60*)

hedgehog is touched, it is capable of moving very quickly (*70*)

but it usually rolls itself into a prickly ball, thus (*80*)

helping to keep its enemies at a safe distance. Although (*90*)

not many people keep them, hedgehogs make very interesting

[pets. (*100*)

10

When I was at school, I always wanted to learn (*10*)

woodwork but, as I was a girl, this was not (*20*)

possible, as woodwork was then regarded as a boy's subject. (*30*)

Today, attitudes have changed and jobs once traditionally

[regarded as (*40*)

male or female are now, in theory, open to either (*50*)

sex, though where the major qualification is sheer physical

[strength (*60*)

most women are effectively eliminated from the outset. Oddly

[enough (*70*)

although boys used to be barred from cookery and sewing (*80*)

classes, men have always been accepted as chefs and dress (*90*)

designers and, indeed, have usually excelled in both these fields. (*100*)